MW00626584

Riverbank: New & Selected Poems

By

Hank Hudepohl

To my family and my friends – for walking with me

© 2021 by Hank Hudepohl

Published by Pine Row Press
107 W Orchard Road
Ft. Mitchell, KY 41011

ISBN: 978-1-7363394-0-4

August 2021

First Edition

10 9 8 7 6 5 4 3 2 1

Cover photo credit: Paul Owens

Publisher's website at pinerow.com

Author's website at hankhudepohl.com

Acknowledgments

Appalachian Heritage (2001)
"Horseshoes"

Cargoes (2005)
"Baskets"

Limestone (2005)
"Relocating"

Ghoti (2005)
"Summer Job"

Image: Word – An Anthology (2005)
"Burning Off"

Cold Mountain Review (2014)
"Summer Camp"

Stonecoast Poetry Review (2014)
"Agave"

Sixfold (2015)
"Crossed Words"
"Riverbank"

"Confidence"
"The Furrier"

Tule Review (2015)
"Retreat"

The Writer's Almanac (2011, 2021)
"The Fair"
"Family Garden"
"The Heavens"

Riverbank: New & Selected Poems

"Be still like a mountain, and flow like a great river."
—Lao Tzu

Riverbank

Come, walk with me along the riverbank
with an old man & his stick, a shadow,
and a boy whistling into an empty bottle
that he found stuck in the soft mud.
The river never looks the same way twice.

The rusted barges float past full of coal.
It is late summer sinking into fall. The river is life,
is earth, is the ground note of an ancient song
if you listen for it. Heraclitus once said
you cannot step into the same river twice.

Let it move you by boat, by raft, by canoe,
by whatever means available to your luck.
Let it carry you away, purify you, inebriate you
with the intoxicating notes of frogs & crickets.
No one ever crosses the same river twice.

The river is daughter & sister, life giver
and lover of sky & bird & fish.

The river is the blood of condensation, of fog,

redeemer of lost ways, collector of light, a thief.

You can never cross the same river twice.

Henry, how long since you've crossed a river?

Artery of disarray, spare parts, rusted cans,

of slatestone, storm-tossed limbs, driftwood,

marshes and grasses, cache of wildflowers: this river

never says my name the same way twice.

All the Lost Hours

Remember? Owls like ghosts in the dark.
We skipped stones by moonlight past curfew.

The secrets we didn't know we held
Spoke themselves, one delicate word

At a time, my hand in yours, the forest
Impossible to navigate.

So, we closed our eyes. We touched the trees
As if blindfolded, we tripped over limbs

And vines, we walked the uneven path.
Had Monet painted us in twilight,

Our bodies would have merged into one
Whitish blur in the gloaming shadows,

A ripple, an echo, an impermanence.
Even your body, when I touched you,
Quivered as though you might disappear.

The Truth About Poetry

You know a few truths:
A hungry dog will bite,
Water and bourbon flow downhill,
The wicked witch isn't dead.

When you are inside a poem
You become the dog,
It may be useful to drink bourbon,
Your inner witch is exonerated.

At the South

In a full moon, by the light of it,
The tree shadows magicked the street
With people, some shadows skinny
as stalks, some fat as pumpkins.

I took a liking to a boy the size of me,
a wisp of shade, missing his right leg
and a part of the middle torso.
His expression was all smiles.

Imagination can play that way when alone,
When a cloud or a long shadow
Looks like a living thing, a leaping horse,
A rabbit, a longed-for, new companion.

I see this now through the telescoping days
of memory, the thought that had no voice
when my best friend moved away. I was six,
He was six, and how can a boy know
When his life is about to change forever?

Light Verse About Cars

Doughnuts, fish tails, u-turns, down-shifting
through all the ways I have driven a car
as I listen to the falling ice tonight

reminds me I am lucky to be alive, lucky
to have swerved and maneuvered my way
through the backroads of Kentucky and puberty,

then later, lucky behind the wheel when I drove
cross country, steering a terrestrial Nova
I nearly crash landed in Oklahoma under starlight

when nodding off the road. Tonight, the jangling keys
of those cars are reticent, the engines cold.
The fascination of what's dangerous has pretty lines,

but that's only part of the allure. It is the actual driving,
sometimes on a breezy evening,
that can soothe you and change your mood forever.

Say, for example, you are a teenager and the girl
next to you is wearing a thin-strapped, sheer white
    dress,
which is the flag of your surrender. She then asks you to
    explore

a philosophical question. You would be obliged to
    consider it.
I have driven a car to games, to funerals,
to the grocery store, to an office countless times.

When I am behind the wheel,
I can always feel the car's savage force.
I possess the absolute, binary certainty

that with each passing exit we are all just a left
or right turn away from the shopping mall
or something else, each of us flirting
with a new destiny as we make our way home.

The Furrier

His years and days and hours are threaded
and wound round the spool into the seam
of the joined hide, pressed there, eyed, sewed up
in a scarf or coat with a fur trim at the neckline.

He says, with a gentleman's wink,
"This will look so wonderful on you, wear it."
And his customers oblige him for hats, scarves,
coats of opossum, otter or the shine of mink.

The sewing machine, branded *Never Stop.*
His one hand over the next stitching
until the bifocaled seams of perfection
are set exquisitely in their proper place.

Anachronistic. Patient. Hopeful.
The spells of time and law are against his ways.
No apprentice now, not even his son
will learn the trade he learned in Istanbul.

"Take a candy," he says, and feeling more bold,
"I will make you a scarf!" He picks off the floor
scraps of farm-raised mink and bends to his task
revived, unashamed, deliberate, and old.

The Sanctity of Pumpkins

Ripe gourd, God's eye of autumn
bound to earth, swelling
among the umbilical of rooted vines.
Which one are you?

A head for the scarecrow? The horseman?

The one stolen from our porch in the dark,
smashed in the street?

The one the roadside farmer sold us
with twisted stem, scar of field dirt
along the lower ribbing?

The one on my front steps, uncut,
water-logged, so bottom-heavy
that when I picked it up it spilled open?

The one we will scrape out with our hands,
pull stringy pulp, grope
the wet nest of seeds?
The one where we will carve out teeth?

The one we will light from the inside?
The one that will stare

like the eyes of my lunatic great uncle,
that hangman, haunt of death? Or just a lit pumpkin
flickering in darkness?

I could say:
There is this moment and nothing more.
I could look away from how, all season long
it gathered shape
from air, from water, from a bedding of soil,
how it came into being.

The tree knows nothing of its shadow.
The pumpkin knows nothing
of its hollowed-out self.
This evening, the cold October air
knows nothing of yellow leaves,
of migrations,
of the needles of frost
that will frock the grass come morning.

Confidence

You know it
when you have it in hand.
The world. And you can become,
without it, so small
as to fit between
the letters of a single word
like if or why.

With it, you can lean casually
upon a capital I. Too much
and you grow so
infinite you believe you can see
the Milky Way
on the back of your nail.
Without any at all,
you will grasp
like a child for an open hand
and fail.

When I was a child, my friends called me by my last name. Summer wasn't a season, it was the unexplored, the wild. All my ambitions could fit in a raindrop.

Blessings

The table is set for family,
like a table of plenty
in the home of Nebuchadnezzar.
The table we wished for,
the one made from barn boards,
emerged out of a catalogue one day
and arrived by postal courier.

Bless it, bless the people around it
and the food upon it. May this table
become, in the years before us,
as worthy and weathered and useful
as the barn it once was.
May it lose its luster, collect nicks
and stray marks, humble
our daily gathering around it.

Remind us to be less perfect but sturdy,
forgiving to the touch
but headstrong about our purpose.
May it bear an eventual likeness
to the one from my childhood
where I sat up late with punishment
well into adolescence
upon refusal of my mother's chicken livers,

among other delicacies,
where she swore with all her heart
to coerce us into gratitude.

I remember how she stood by the stove
in a faint haze of cigarette smoke,
stranded in routine between her life
and ours, doing, in fact, what a mother will do,
starve you as well as feed you,
which is to prepare you for your time to leave,
and then when you are finally gone
cry because of it.

Summer Camp

Locker packed, pink, pirouetting on the driveway
on its wheels, pulled toward the car.
Time to go, to let go, familiar slap of screen door,
slap of your sister's small hand against your back. Hugs.
    Goodbyes.

Letter from you on Post-it notes.
A few words here and there: "miss you", "send me more
    sheets"
on pastel colored squares
and then the bomb: "get me out of here."

Not a bomb but a cold numb
sense of you gone. The stillness of it all,
still as your bed, sheets tucked in,
only the morning light disturbing it.

Summer camp, not some state
of political upheaval. Tank tops, top dogs,
dog hot days, starry nights, whispers, jokesters,
leave behinds. Carefree, free will, the willies,
a meadow of forget-me-nots. Let go.

Two hazy weeks. The morning pick up arrives.
She walks with her cabin mates down hill

toward me waving, would be running to catch her
but I play cool too. "How was it?"
"So far down it was up," she thumbs.

Backpack, track back, pack up.
Her splinted finger already on the mend.
Friends at every turn. Bye Lucy, bye Jen.
Hugs for Stacy. Where's Maggie? Panic, tears,

now calm again. The wind moves like this –
shakes the leaves, runs barefoot through grass,
holds tight to stray things.
I move alongside her toward the car.

The sun shines like a cataract of fall.
All the summer swaying leaves
surround us, their richest greens going brown
following our way back home.

Wrestling with the Bear

Wrestling with my dad as a child was to wrestle with a bear. Except this bear, instead of eating you on Saturday morning, would lay on top of you in the bed and squish your head into a pile of pillows, or else twist your arm behind your back until you said uncle or mercy. Even if you begged and pleaded, the sweet moment of being released from the Grip of Ultimate Suffering didn't come swiftly, because a bear does not get up swiftly, it lumbers upward in the same slow-motion way it lumbered down. You can actually feel each bone in your back cracking as he rolls off you, pushing you further down into the mattress as he rises up, and sometimes in the process of getting up, you feel him crushing your ankle or maybe your entire leg as a minor casualty of being set free. But on the upside, his plodding along style makes it easy for you to counter attack if you so dare. That counter attack, especially if delivered to the blind side, must be accompanied by a swift and sure exit from the room, preferably down the stairs and out the door for the remainder of the day. If that route is not possible, a reasonable alternative is to hide in your sister's cubby, located under a desk and recessed into a wall, well out of reach of The Bear. Otherwise, the result of capture is doubly disastrous and can result in such torture as the Charlie Horse, or worse, the Arm Pit head lock or the dreaded Bad Breath lay upon with whiskers. I survived these encounters, if only just, and they taught me a few things about how to bend a finger or bite an arm. Even more than that, they prepared me for a weekend morning with my own kids, tied up in knots in bed or on the floor, twisting each other into raw pretzels of mercy, deep in the agony of our own laughter.

Apples
after Robert Frost

This is an apple picking day
when scents of apple mix with hay,
and apple-full limbs hang so low
that all my work is turned to play.

I touch a branch, it scares a crow.
The orchard trees seem stoic though.
I fill my pail with orbs of red,
and take my share before I go.

My hands are worn, and where fruit bled
they smell of apples harvested.
And underneath the fertile trees,
the earth is apple carpeted.

But still the sight I long to see
as dusk turns this grove shadowy
is when the night fills sky and tree
so full of lights it startles me.

August Night, A Meeting

My neighbor called me out of my house
with that gentleman's way of speaking

in the South, his voice full of iron
and charm. So I went over to where

he beckoned me from the street curb,
some part of restrained gallop in the way

his words urged me to gather around him,
something he wanted me to see,

some *thing* he could not lift or touch
or call by name. That's how I arrived

and stood beside him, staring hard
at a dark rope in a gutter of concrete.

"Copperhead," he said without looking up.
I watched him prod it with a metal rake,

its flat head glistening in the dark water
of blood. I wanted him to hammer it again

to prove to me it was dead. "Copperhead,"

he said once more, "through and through."

Locusts scratched at the dark. The wooded
night surrounded us with small voices.

Then I heard him say, as I turned to leave,
"Where there's one there's two."

Baskets

My mother kept the family laundry basket on our second
floor.
Yellow wicker, round, big enough to hide in, a place to
disappear

then jump out again to scare my sister. Weekdays I'd lob in
my dirty shirts, my socks, my underwear. I'd watch them
disappear

over the lip into the basket's soft darkness, where they'd
land
on a cushion of clothes. By weekend, we wanted the
whole pile to disappear.

I'd go outdoors then to the woods, a dusty ball field, the
deep end of a pool.
At night, we'd hunt each other with flashlights. We wore
black to disappear.

Imagine the catcher's mitt is a basket, I told myself before
each pitch.
But when my fastball hit the batter's back, he fell. I wanted
to disappear.

My sister made out in our living room after school. I shot

baskets on the patio.

When I tried to watch from behind the couch, she stared at me. Disappear.

One summer afternoon, the basket of a hot air balloon bumped our neighbor's roof.
Two men looked down at me. A flame roared. The basket rose up, then disappeared.

"Henry, empty the laundry basket." I wished for a grown-up's life free of chores.
No one ever told me how childhood loves us, deceives us, then disappears.

Burial Ground

Beyond the fence, headstones: angular
and pale against a backdrop of leafshade,

jutting up out of uneven, mossy ground
in skewed angles, sunlit gray. Pines taller

than oaks bordered the fence, and inside,
cone-bearers had thrust straight trunks

up through the dappled cluster of graves.
Long needles flecked the ground. Chiseled

on gravestones, two names: Clay and Hatfield.
My grandpa walked off to a far end

and looked up into a bewilderment of trees.
"This place has calm," he said,

one hand in his denim jacket, the other resting
on the holster of a gun. He said it almost

to himself. I thought he was showing me
where to bury him. I didn't answer –

I was studying the faces in the graves.

The Thrill of Catching

line-drives, short hops, stingers
off the end of the coach's fungo
slapped me out of sleep
after school, all of us school-tired

and jumpy as the baseballs
that skittered over a dirt and rock infield.
We fielded ground balls
until our bodies ached from bending,

until the purfling of dusk
hemmed the field with indigo
and turned us into shadows.
In that spell of dark coming on

the bone-white skin of the ball
looked luminous as a small moon
that we batted, gloved, tossed
to one another like young gods

who had forgotten they were boys
out late again, playing a game
that must come to an end,
all of us, for the moment, connected

to the outfielder running deep
for a fly ball, following the curve
of flight with his body, seeing the final
point of that ghostly arc vanish
into the dark web of his glove.

Heirlooms? They surround me like silence and dust. I do not disturb them.

Surprise

A child can find it
anywhere.
Even the inside
curve
of a spoon can hold
it quietly,
like perfection,
where
at the breakfast table
she stared
deep
into her upside
down reflection.

First Snow

I never saw such darkness
broken, such shingle-shine

on farm roofs sloped in sleep.
The whiteness of it all,

a moon saddling the sky,
the whiteness of not a single

blemish on the linen tablecloth.
White as fingers of frost

at the kitchen window, and clear
as icicles fixed to the chrome

fender of my parent's car. Once
upon a time, we broke ice in mittens,

daggered the melt in our mouths
and laughed through winter fangs.

Burning Off

after Andrew Wyeth

Horse and hay smell, barn must, the moist
residues of mid-morning, his hands

roughed up beyond youthful recognition
by farm tools, neglect, years of holding

on for the next harvest, big hauls, the home
he hoped for but never had. Sweat stains

the bridle hung by a hook on the wall.
Looking out, he sees meadow mist thinning

away to nothing under the sun, a ruse
of substance like a promise broken.

A birth that comes by surprise also
breaks promises, the mare stalled behind him

shows this. He rinses hands in bucket water.
In the bloodied hay, a foal, born early, kicks.

Passage

A leaf – small, oblong,
yellowed – circling downward
lands on autumn's disc
of light, the lake, an equilibrium
tilting leeward toward winter.

The silver boat waits,
pulled on shore, oars jutting out,
braced against the bank.
Metal sides shine
bright as fish scales.

Leaves drop into
the boat's empty belly,
where only yesterday
it held the whole summer, my dad,
and shoulder-high between us
that cold, orange enormity
of a setting sun.

Fairy Tales

This is where it begins and ends:
me, downstairs, nursing old wounds
late into the evening, far too late

for redemption or even for a last
moment of clear-minded reflection,
she, in bed, head on pillow, sleeping

or sleepless, fixed to one side
by a feeling growing inside her,
something about to happen, a change

that sobers me into the night, alert.
I am restless, not from cars slipping
through these wet, narrow streets

much too fast, not from hollow chimes
assailed by the wind outdoors,
not from the anvil in my head I strike

again and again with the same thoughts
like a smithy beating metal for the sparks.
Our baby is coming. The whole world

tilts and we are on it. I am restless

with wonder, wondering if I am enough
for her, wondering if I can give her
a better life, wondering if her eyes are blue.

Joy

There is green in the air by the sea.
The sea green air sings a blue song
and the gulls dive through it.

A man or woman is not a single wave,
but upon the wave in the beard
of sea foam I have seen a man laugh,

And in the belly wave of a woman,
the sea laughs and sings the singular blue
song that hums with life renewing.

I hear it now – the wind like water
in the leaves, my feet in a sea of dirt
drifting miles away from the ocean.

I sway, I sway, this new song
of life swings in my arms like a child born
and belly laughing above the blue.

Farm Road

after Andrew Wyeth

You follow the girl, her back turned. She bares
nothing to the voyeur's eye but possession itself,

the nape of her neck left naked to the sun.
The day is getting on. She walks a step ahead

of you on a farm road untellable from the hill
she has to climb. The hillside is browned out

but for a few distant trees that bear leaves still.
She is coated, straight-backed, and resolute.

You only see her from the shoulders up.
Her hair is divided into two woven braids

and lustrous as the sheen on autumn's acorn.
It is not spring and you are not invited

to know the shape of her mouth, the lines
on the palms of her hands, the slender path

between her breasts. Does she even sense
that you are close enough to grab her

from behind if you wanted to, or touch her
shoulder and ask her one more time not to go?

It is wrong to want her, knowing, as you must,
that she is not your wife and years younger,

that the day will only grow colder, the night
will come, the trees will go bare in time.

Das ist verboten. Men have cheated before
and will cheat again. And yet who can deny

an impulse as free as the wisps of her hair?
If she turned around, you would know wet cheeks

or her smile, or else scorn, telling you to go away
and never come again. She walks ahead

and rising before her is this dark wave of land
that shadows us all.

Fishing

Say fishing and I think of the bait:
nightcrawlers in a cup of dirt tangled

up in each other, that ooze black blood
when I sink a hook in them;

or metal lures lined up in the tackle box,
bright colors, except for that pale green one

twice as long as my finger with six hooks
dangling from its belly and red dots for eyes;

or a yellow tube of catfish bait we never used.
I like the idea of early morning by the lake

just before the day happens, when the surface
is cold silver, a light fog's suspended in air

and even the birds are asleep. I go there
to cast myself out on a thread, and wait.

Sunshine has a way of warming the skin and the soul.

Family Garden

Tell me again about your garden.
    Tell me how you planted, in the small
        flat of mountain land, corn seed

And bean seed, how your finger poked the soil
    then you dropped in three dark bean seeds
        for every yellow seed of corn.

Trees and mountains collared your land,
    but the fenced garden opened freely
        to sun and warm summer rains.

Your potato rows bulged in July. You ached
    from digging them up, your hands down in dirt,
        the cool lump of a tuber, brown-spotted,

Just recovered, a greeting, like shaking hands.
    Baskets full of bumpy brown potatoes filled
        your basement until fall, until you gave

Away what you could, throwing out the rest.
    You gave away honey from the white hive too,
        that box of bees beside the garden,

Honey stored in Mason jars, a clearest honey
　　　　nectar from lin tree blossoms and wild flowers.
　　　　　　The bright taste of honey on the tongue

Spoke of the place, if a place can be known
　　　　by the activity of bees and a flavor in the mouth,
　　　　　　if a person can be known by small acts

Such as these, such as the way you rocked
　　　　summer evenings from a chair on the porch
　　　　　　tending your inner garden, eyes closed.

Flower Talk

I walk along happy streets, their long paths
draped with dogwood blooms and clean hedgework.
I am the worrier carrying a pocket of winter twigs,
careless with my thoughts. Daffodils blaze up

in rows, their cupped petals a totem to spring,
their slender stalks as limber as hope herself.
"Cheer up" they seem to say as I pass by
(they know they must speak plainly to me)

for this is the most obvious thing they could say
to the rain. Or else they could say "Kiss me,"
which is what the rain does to them later
in a downpour, the kind of rain without reckoning.

For the Child of a Miner

Coal miner, dark and mad,
hacking out his time, caught in the mountain.
Black coal dust, choked up and spit out.

Raise the steel again.
My father fought it, lean and stubborn framed,
twenty-two years making tunnel space —

cold, empty matter. One gray-lit morning
I watched from my window his stiff walk,
scratch of field grass against his pants,

a loose lunch pail clamped by a fist.
Head bent, hair hanging forward,
he was taking bites from a biscuit
and aiming straight for that hollow mine.

Gathering Up Leaves With My Daughter

My mid-fall yard,
leaf river of rust,
shimmers and flows
from gust to gust.

Leaf-wet shadows
where, bending, I rake
smell of wood-must
and summer's ache.

I build small piles
that scatter and sail,
then rake again
to no avail.

My daughter asks,
as she brings more leaves,
will I put them
back on the trees?

Gridiron

We carried a swarm of noise to the basement
after school, busting the locker room

before practice, jostling, shouting jokes
above the slam of lockers. Coach roamed

the aisles, "Let's move, let's move," a ball cap
hiding his eyes. We taped up, cinched cleats

like our fathers once did, like theirs before.
My locker mate ate aspirin without a sip

of water. The bathroom stalls were doorless.
When coach blew his whistle, it split you.

"Outside!" We gripped our helmets by the mask
and hit the stairs, each of us filing through

a tunnel that rose and led us squinting onto grass,
boys who believed they could conquer their past.

Summer Ice

We lined up in the candy shop's shelter
        as heat lacquered the tar-hot streets.

Teenage girls lingered in bikini tops,
        tan, lip-glossed, too cool to notice anything

but their own reflection in shop windows.
        I sat on a bench out front with my brother

where we bent over our cups of flavored ice.
        Yellow jacket bees hovered near a spill

of red syrup. I shooed them away from me.
        We ate hunkered down in that mid-summer

just before I left home, too nonchalant
        to care about whether or not it ever rained,

or who would be going where in a few days,
        or where I stood in relation to my few dollars

and cents, or about all that would surprise me
        years later with the sting of consequence.

Little Blue Springs Holler

From the porch of the trailer looking out
we could see how the holler narrowed to a V

where two mountain ridges closed the gap we lived in.
The steep slope of trees hid the sun from view

until mid-morning, when we'd spot it climbing out
over the hilltop slowly, griddle-hot and close.

By late afternoon, the sun disappeared over the other
ridge
and the woods were lost in shadow once again.

The sun never brought me peace or set me thinking,
but O when the moon showed up over the trees at night

it felt as if God himself was looking in
with his one, big, inquisitive eye.

Craftsmanship

Take, for instance, this book in my hand,
a prop to back a blank page,
poems about Michelangelo,
a man who said he carved by clearing away,
who reached into darkness for shapes
that reached out to him.
The forms rose from marble
the way a body surfaces from a wading pool.

Imagine working with chisel and rasp,
rescuing the rock's face one flake at a time,
seeing the surprise of those pleading eyes
meet yours in that first encounter,
an abiding faith
in your ability to render a body whole,
to free it from life's inscrutable abyss.

How can you save the grief,
the folds of her heavy robes, and in her lap,
the arched body and neck of her lifeless son?

Or is she sculpting you?
And how can these words, like flakes of stone
against a flat page, that raise and etch a life,
tell both a lie and a truth?

Excursion

Let's walk the path by Moye convent
where a nun surprised me once
by asking, "Did you find what you were looking for?"

Here the trees stand in red and yellow coats
around a field so cold
it cracks beneath our feet.

The hour is past harvest time
and bitterness hangs in the air.
Horses linger here, then steer our way

when we dangle a handful of straw
through barbed wire. A black filly eases over,
smelling peppermint in your hand.

Hold it for your sake like this:
open, flat, palm up, fingers extended.
She will not bite you, this girl

with her muzzle between the wires,
here for the morning offering.
Her tongue is warm and rough,
her teeth like clicking stones.

The eyes are the sky
Of tomorrow
The hands are the sea
And this single thought –
I am not yet done –
Is the sun.

Horseshoes

Horseshoe pitching is a way of life.
I remember my grandfather,

the hard iron rubbed and tucked
firm into the pocket of his hand,

a dangling cigarette between loose lips,
taking proud and careful aim

at an iron stake slanting from a sandy pit
some thirty feet away. He cradled

that shoe before him like a newborn
and with an underhanded fling,

turned the heavy horseshoe loose and
answered with a high clenched hand

the jarring cry of the stake's shrill ring.

The Fair

Before the gates opened, before popcorn
        and cotton candy drifted down throats

like sweet and salty summer evenings
        of childhood, before the townspeople

confessed to the music and lights,
        the ferris wheel baskets swung empty

in a slow arc, one by one, offering color
        to the sky – red, yellow, orange, blue.

Just roving boys, what else could we do
        but follow the sandaled feet of girls

out to the fair to buy them rides
        until our pockets turned up penniless,

until we lost them in the dark
        the way sparrows will fly from you,

until our last walk past the fun house
        mirrors stretched our bodies like gum,

when we caught ourselves looking
        back at ourselves for the first time.

Glassblower

No single flame, just a steady gold eye
of stove, an opening large enough to throw
a well-aimed baseball into oblivion,
the gate to furnace fire called the glory hole.
This is where the Blower turns the hot glass
"like a ball of honey" he says, and lifts it to show
the syrup ooze on the far end of a pole,
his forearms flexing, the molten glass aglow
on the puntee, alive in hues of green and red.
When he sets it on an iron plate and beats it fast
with vice and jacks, my daughter whispers,
"I see a jellyfish." His cheeks full, he blows
through the end of the rod and the glass balloons
into a ripe, round apple, hot and sweet.

American Gothic

after Grant Wood

Some say he's eccentric: he washes the house
every spring, eats three raw eggs at first light,
rubs the side of his head when he talks.

He snores so loudly they sleep in separate rooms.
She can't stand his temper or his groping hands
like weasels in the hen house at night.

She writes poems about this and other matters:
the thunder of a moth against the kitchen screen,
the frail heads of her mother's frost-bitten roses,

the hours of silence baked into her breads.
Nothing grows inside unless she commands it.
What happens outside is God's business.

Nightfall in Roanoke

She sleeps in the crib, rustling sheets
    as she stirs and shifts positions
        like the silky rustle of pin oak leaves

outside my open window this evening.
    By daylight, I saw the same leaves glisten
        in their greenness, so new, yellow-hued

and glinting in the full sun of spring.
    I sat on the porch holding my daughter,
        watching this hillside in Virginia brim

and tremble with light like that first woodland
    could have when the center of all things budded.
        Now, the day ends with me in bed, tossing

in the middle of my life, as our world rests
    upon oceans and spins with stars in space.
        My daughter stirs again. I will go to her

in the dark if she cries. I will watch her sleep.
    Outside, trunks standing in the woods
        twist and grow, rooted in their place.

Rockhouse Mountain

By six a.m., coal trucks are piping smoke trails
up our mountain road, spinning loose gravel

with large, rubber wheels, winding up higher
through the trees. Their headlamps are two cold eyes

which vanish in the dark then reappear
suddenly, up to take a noiseless breath

from you with their snake turning. By eight,
the sun filters through gray dust plumes

tossed behind the charge of rock haulers.
Look how they mount the ridge

on their knuckles, always inching ahead
to break the top, angled slightly forward,
eager to dare you with a lower gear.

Starlight

And suddenly it was as if we stood
in the middle of the night sky
at that moment
when the galaxy of your womb
appeared on the monitor
before us
made visible by waves of sound.

We glimpsed the hidden and unknown
mystery of your belly,
a universe of new life
deep in your center.
The doctor pointed out the brighter objects
in the dark screen,
things he thought worth seeing,
with names of scientific origin
like the names of constellations or distant worlds.

I thought of a time back when,
through a telescope,
I watched the far-off stars
emerge out of the sky
so high over the hills
it made my head spin:
Orion, lacerta, corvus,

and ursa major which amateurs like me
call the big dipper.

And here I am star-gazing again
looking into you
by ultrasound
thinking about outer space and creation,
discovering uterus, ovary,
the fallopian tubes,
and still as wide-eyed
as when I first made a connection
with the stars.

I am speechless for
there, in the center of your galaxy,
the brightest star burns
and grows brighter,
a new-found constellation of light
waiting for a name
but just as luminous without one.

Sometimes in my life I drifted like the cotton of a milkweed seed on a breeze.

Summer Job

While my manager chain-smoked Camels
in the closet,
I rubbed my knuckles to an icy raw
against the stainless steel freezer case,
leaning in
to scrape out the buckets
for one scoop or two,
the line trailing out the door.

Money changed hands between me
and the insatiable beast,
its tail always regenerating,
its head reddened, balding, always
in my face, making demands

while outside in the streets,
the parking meter
was busy running out of magic again,
my car without the inner resources
or good looks
to talk its way out of a ticket,
my wages not enough to pay the fines.

On breaks, I was the glutton
eating scoop after scoop, drinking

thick malts until my head ached.
I was the soda jerk,
the proverbial fool who would be damned
not to get his fill.

The Dinner Bell

"I'm the Daddy," I hear
myself say,
rebuffing her sass,
telling her to sit back down

at the dinner table
like good children do:
keep your feet off the chair,
sit up straight,
don't clang your fork again
and again against the rim of the china plate.

She likes the way it rings
the ears, needle sharp and true,
splitting through whatever we were saying
or had planned to say,
(as her infant sister cries)

tuning up the night with her treble fork
until we find her among us
again, at last,
this wide-eyed, knowledgeable
all-of-the-sudden big sister
who is only three –
and we obey.

The Pocketknife

My grandfather's pocketknife –
he could bring it to life on reflex,
flick it open to help me
slice an apple or cut a string.

Its heft in my hand feels awkward
as the word *heirloom* in my mouth,
mute in my pocket as a roll of dimes.
I am not ready for this.

The blades look shiny
and dangerous. They mean it.
The crevice still holds a piece of lint
from his jean pocket.

Engraved on the front: stainless
just as it is in my mind,
stainless and perfect,
the implacable knife in his hand

floating in memory now,
saving me from what I can't see coming,
a blade like Beowulf's
flashing against the dark.
The light-tongued.

The pocket-jewel.
The dance-of-steel.
The metal-tooth.
The silver-switch.
The take-your-breath.

Retreat

In memory of J.F.H.

A mountain top, a trail head,
a pine-encircled cabin
silhouetted in silence, an ice-cold lake,
the dock on the lake, cattails on the shore
leaning toward collapse,

the swollen ring of frogs at evening
calling you back,
all the places you ever went
to get away,
are not so solitary, no,

not when I think of
your soft-handed goodbye at the airport gate,
the hospital garage, the dark garden
of your swollen eyes,

and later,
a private room with folded white sheets
sitting neatly on the corner of your empty bed.

The Heavens

Watching the night sky for the Pleiades meteor shower
from the back porch, nothing above but clouds and
    airplanes,

bug bites at our ankles, a sudden track of headlights
against the house, pet eyes peering out a window.

"Not a meteor in sight," I say aloud to my daughters
and the nothingness above us, both of them standing

on the picnic table leaning back into me
like two armfuls of warm laundry, asking me about the
    night,

wondering what do stars look like up close?
where does the sky begin? how long does it take to get
    there?

while I hold them close to me in a patch of backyard
in America, my wristwatch illuminating

the hour, my thoughts lost in the gap of time
between this night and forever, these wonders in
    whispers,

the heavens so near, questions so simple,
and the answers so far beyond my knowing.

Two Modes of Harvesting

Today I am gathering rice
by canoe.
It is quiet except
for my oar dipping
into the water,

the river sluicing
along the sides of my boat,
droplets dripping from the paddle.
A snake swims
by the port side
making curves in the water
as it goes.

I reach the rice plants
along the shore.
The grassy stalks rasp
against the sides of the boat.
I bend them slightly
over the gunwale
to shake loose the dark grains
where they pile
around my bare feet
like offerings.
Not even the alligator

stirs.

But the truth is
I am not in a boat
harvesting rice.
I am like you, maybe,
navigating the aisles
of a grocery store
with a cart and its shoddy wheel,
looking again
with my own two hands
for something to eat.

Relocating

My ninety-year-old grandmother, chin-deep
in a plate of splintered lobster shells,

sits across from me. She winces as she clamps
her vise on another red claw. The claw cracks

and splatters. She peels back the shell
to get at the white meat. Her fingers shake

with delight. I know how this night will end
for the lobster. I drive my grandmother

to the retirement home afterward. The mid-west
evening is breezy, warm. I help her to the door.

She says she can smell the ocean. She says
she can still remember. She calls me

by my father's name. "You mustn't move away,"
she says. She kisses the back of my hand.

Villanelle for a Teacher

after Seamus Heaney

I heard you were back in the States.
You who had kindly shepherded and cheered
Me forward into poetry. You who had extended a hand.

I looked it up – the dates, the readings, the words –
Following you back across the pages, the years.
I heard you were back in the States.

You moved like a sort of migratory bird:
Chicago. Cincinnati. Buffalo. Ithaca. Maybe here?
Poetry flew fast-forward. You were the steady hand.

I scanned websites for a word, an omen, a place
To have a chance encounter, a scorpion bowl or beer.
I heard you were back in the States.

Maybe once I had promise. Maybe once I heard
The distant thunder of a train rise then disappear
Like poetry moving forward. You steadied my hand.

In middle age, the frosts and tests are hard.
I am fool to miss the gates, the books, your good cheer.
I heard you were back in the States.
Move me again into poetry. Steady my shaking hand.

All Rivers Flow West

Out west, pueblo villages.
Out west, adobe worn to curves.
Out west, a dwelling.
Leaning against the porch wall, a guitar.
Beside it, violet flowers
overflowing a clay pot.
I stayed there once, just passing through
and remained for over two years.
Out west, days seemed longer.

The proprietor said to me,
"Call me Tia.
Usted es siempre agradable en mi casa."
The small garden of her backyard
won a prize
and was tended by a skinny man from Tijuana
who knew his annuals
and said nothing in English.

I slept well among the flowers
and the book-lined walls of her home.
Paintings hung in every room,
colorful scenes of the countryside
or else glimpses of Mexico City.
Out west, warm nights, maize and topaz.

Out west, armadillos.
Out west, Coronado looking for the city of gold.

She owned a bookstore where I sometimes worked.
It was serious business. In fact,
she mixed Australian honey and tetracycline
as a cocktail for her ulcers.
But in the evening, on the verandah,
she preferred a glass of chardonnay.

Tia did not talk of her divorce.
She was bilingual and a dual citizen.
Her Mexican friends forgave her
for these and other discretions,

such as sharing Cinco de Mayo with gringos
or falling behind on news of Marcos.
Her sister was murdered in Mexico City
but her son still lived nearby.
He brought his children to her house
whenever his wife allowed.

Occasionally, when the mood struck Tia,
she'd hire a guitar player from Ensenada
who drove for four hours to play and sing
Mexican love songs all evening
while people wandered among the books.

Some of them even sat with us
in a semi-circle around him
and dreamed a little.

"I am so tired these nights,"
Tia said to me near the time that I left.
I believed her.
I said, "Tia, when you are traveling
You are always welcome in my house."

The other day
I heard news from out west:
Tia of the flowers had died.
From where I stand now
all rivers flow west.
The sky here does not move.

Out west, a silence.
Out west, the Anasazi too have vanished.
At evening, when I am alone on the porch,
the sun draws my eyes in that direction.

My Tia had a beach home in Zihuatanejo.
She inherited it from her family
and once invited me there for New Year's
but I didn't go.
I can imagine her there now,

sitting on the porch, facing
the ocean's interminable surf
and the scorpion-hot sand,
one hand holding a book and the other holding
down the unruly, buffeted page.

Sometimes you have to say to life:
I'd like a re-evaluation.

A Night Passing

This is not sleep.
Eight hours tossing on a bunk
below the flight deck of an aircraft carrier.
I am alone, untouchable,
celled in all night under covers,
disconnected from the moonlight
gathering above me. All night

gray metal planes
float down toward the ship
as though on unseen cables.
Each plane emerges out of the darkness
rigid and stark, sleek-lined,
with a single light to guide it home
like an open eye descending.

I remember how on summer nights
I watched from my bedroom window
bats in our backyard
flashing and flicking
over the swimming pool,
shadows moving faster than my eyes.
All angle and wing,
the bats would nose-dive to the pool's surface,
skimming the water

just close enough to dip their tongues.

An aircraft strikes the flight deck, jerked
to a sudden stop by hook and wire.
I flinch. My bunk shakes with the blow.
The thin line between hit and miss
is barely visible.
I lie awake tonight.
I cannot see what is moving in
or out of the darkness.

Solitude

Snow and ice blister the field.
This is not your farm,
these are not your winds
twisting the edges of trees.

Here, in the calm circle of the house,
where light drifts in and out
of a front-yard clearing like a timid stranger,
you become attuned to the stubble

of wintered corn stalks, raggedy-like
in the field. And then you see the brunt shadow
of this weather upon an actual man
walking the road past the house:

poorly clothed, roughly whiskered,
down on his luck today, collar up,
trespassing on your little piece of salvation.

Agave

This morning I woke shot through
with grief and something else
like light breaking
through a skin of clouds.
It was too faint to be a hallelujah –

it seemed instead an assertion
or an admission.
Are we not taught to prepare
the way for good news,
for laughter,
for occasional exciting brushes
against an arm or cheek,
for deliverance from our fate
in a moment of disbelief?

This morning I woke broken
and unyielding.
In waking, I had become
something like the agave plant
outside my window
so many years ago that bloomed once
then fell apart.

I am sending up,

at long last,
a flowering yellow heart.

Crossed Words

I wonder, looking at the red-headed bird at the feeder,

if it is a woodpecker, or cardinal, or maybe a rare, hot-

> headed

warbler come to dine with me on my parent's deck

as I visit with them for a long weekend. I am picking

over the seeds on my plate too, curious about how

I got here, which is to say, living a thousand miles away

and now just a rare visitor to their empty nest,

while my convalescent mom sleeps off her dizziness

in the back bedroom and my dad calls out to me

from the kitchen again to ask if I'd like anything more.

Yes, maybe to understand how migrations, digressions,

even casual addictions can lead to the brink of confusion

where simple questions like "what do you want to eat?"

and "when can you visit again?" can be as complicated to

> answer

as my dad's Sunday crossword, locked as I am in my own

> state

of surprise, my children awaiting my return like Christmas,

my office chair awaiting my shape, my car awaiting my

    key,

my lips in search of a seven-letter word that rhymes with

    why.

Night Watch

I lie awake and question
my deep water.

The watchman in me searches,
wants to know

what is behind stars
and below the ship's hull,

wants to know
what is moving beyond the net

of my hand,
the hook of my eye.

Mountain Morning

This morning the crow and warbler rise early
And annotate the day.
The mountains hide long shadows
And purple flowers. The laurel abounds,
The dense green leaf canopy abounds,
The multitude of insects abound.
All the sun's rays have a purpose here.
All the leaves have a purpose and the grasses too.
The perplexities of these woods,
Your senses, and the confusion of your senses
does not change this.
The misunderstandings and the inattention,
And the scrutiny of people does not change this fact.
The morning comes as a greeting and a prayer.
You have a purpose too.
You are a new morning on a new day.
The flowers do not lament yesterday.
The trees do not grieve what has already happened
Or what may happen still.
The life force of the forest does not consider
the portent of summer sun or a cold rain.
Birds are calling from the darker shadows of trees
And in the sunny openings, birds are calling.
The wood thrush sings with two voices.
In the stillness of an upper slope, in the clearing,

A wild turkey enters then disappears.
Above it all, a hawk circles on and on and on.

Middle School

The preparation of clothes, lunches
made from salad greens and green grapes,
combing the sun-streaked hair of summer
long and straight, lip gloss, eighth grade.

The first day of school was our awakening
like a back slap after the slow days of summer,
the sleeping in, clouds of thoughts
passing over like forgetfulness, harmless.

But now you are making a beeline back to us
from the bus stop, first-day floral dress
flowing, hair falling into your eyes,
the door wide-open, shouting "my bus pass!"

across the kitchen, sparking the place alive again
by your whirlwind return, like the swoop
of morning jays that startle the yard,
a color wheel in motion, and with card in hand

you leave us for school a second time, the bus,
the chatter of friends, the red brick building
of another year, turning down hallways that witness
the fleeting footfalls of your passing through.

What life is, or was, or will be – start it now.

Things I Have Discovered in My Infant's Mouth

A fistful of playsand. The fat
head and stick-end of a tack.
A white paint fleck. Two long
wisps of her mother's hair.
A spotted pebble from the stoop.
A dulled penny. An orange
cheese shaving. A dissolved
shred of paper towel. The three
of diamonds. A domino.
My teeth-marked finger. Her sister's
favorite doll. My cell phone
(call in progress). A twist
of vine from a pumpkin.
Pureed broccoli bits. Blades
of grass. A yellowed maple leaf.
The beginnings of vowels.
Her mother's rosy,
milk-wet nipple.

Beach Play

Waves with sound so soft it turns circles in my ear
Until I can hear the conical shape of tomorrow, of time.

Time to wave goodbye, hello, come again. Hinges creak
With each in and out through the patio screen door.

Another door, a whimsical door opens a path into my id
That runs like honey through the bottom of my feet.

Metrical feet, athlete's foot, sasquatch with big feet:
All memories and maybes, my childhood's dream
    recipe.

"Recipe for disaster" my sour roommate once said
When he saw me in the street kissing his ex.

X marks the spot, an x on my forehead, a treasure map,
Or else a letter in a book, and traced here in the sand.

"Henry, the sand dollars are everywhere" my mom calls
As we dig with our toes in the low tide, waist-deep.

Deep in winter, we bleach them white, place them
On our Christmas tree. On the outside, the pattern of a
    star

Like the Star of Bethlehem. On the inside, five white doves,
And four holes through the middle, one for every nail.

"Nailed it" I brag as the line drive off my bat hits the surf
And I round the beach-towel bases one last time for home.

Bee Pollen

It takes the life of two bees to make
a teaspoon of honey. I see how small
are my accomplishments as I dip
a dense spoonful of their finer breath
& spirit into my green tea. When I stir,
I can almost hear the hum of wings,
see their strict purpose flying in lines
across the meadow of deepest thoughts,
legs heavy with nectar of clover & lavender,
warmed by the summer sun. At night,
they come to me again, sleepless & fervent,
building comb after comb of dream
while I free fall with a bee's heart,
eager to seize flowers by the throat.

Road Work

Down the middle
of the wooded

road two yellow
lines painted on

black top glow
in smoky dusk.

The paint is new.
I can almost smell

the end of summer
off nearby trees.

The painted road
disappears in both

directions. Which
way is my dog-

gone dream? Where
are you, Beatrice?

Departure

The staircase rail, smooth
from the passing grasp of years
and our wood-worn hands.

The Salamander

On a rock wall where I sit, a salamander
turns toward me, its sleek shape dark

and small, quick as my surprise. I stay still.
It pauses an arm's length away. Its black

back glistens like liquid, the body unreal
as a river at rest.

                           Long ago, I caught one
with my bare hands, held it in the cave

of cupped palms like a living verb.
Its body did not stop writhing. Small feet

tickled me before it nosed between fingers
and got away.

                   This one watches me, alert
as reflex, dwelling in the periphery

of encounter. Then in a twitch it is gone
over the ledge, gone before I can gather

my old self, before I can reason, gone
like the loose swing of summer, dirt fields,
the way we all ran home when our mothers called.

Wintering With the Mandans

"The mercury at sunrise stood at 20° below 0."
—William Clark, December 30, 1804

Ice sheathed us in.
We huddled in our huts,
rabbits for a long winter,
gaunt under fur blankets.
Sometimes I ventured out
in the morning, rangy
and curious before light,
a few seeds in my pocket.
Even then, no footprint
fell without their knowing.

Inside earthen lodges,
women gave men warmth.
Where I walked, young scouts
watched me move. They
had names I did not know,
faces I could not see.
In the corral, under glint
of new day glow, horses
snorted, shuddered in cold
and snow, nowhere to go.

Where do you go when you must find your place of timelessness?

Navigating the Shoreline

I could do far worse than spend a life
Or an afternoon in a patch of earth, a field,
This half-acre of marshland fronting the sea,
Watching the tall grasses on the dunes
Lean away and away from the breezes
Then playfully sway back,
Drift upright, then lean over again.
And here, in the curls and mud folds of earth
Where I sit, rivulets of water turn and trickle
In little silver veins of flow,
Rivers at their own scale, drawing me in
And down, but just as soon as they do I see,
far above, the full moon's glow in a blue sky.

Fun at a New England Beach

Swimsuits, towels, sunblock, chairs,
beach umbrella, water.
Pack the car and say a prayer
I don't forget my daughter.

The beach is bright, the sand looks hot
but the drive has turned us sour.
We circle round the parking lot
for close to half an hour.

The sound of surf now greets the ear
a rumbling, roaring din,
like pack mules loaded down with gear
we search for journey's end.

Pitch umbrella, lay out towels
lather on the lotion.
The music booming near our spot
sorta drowns out the ocean.

Here's a wave, don't take her under!
My girl, five years, is bold.
She runs into the ocean surf
Then runs back out – it's cold.

Cold enough to cool us off
and numb us to our knees.
This beach is where it's at, my friend,
to catch a burn and freeze.

The sun dips down, the day is done
We gather up our keep.
Her skin is flecked with salt and sand,
The kind that brings on sleep.

Morning Commute

The morning commute unfolds in front of me,
parade in fantastic colored stripes
across the street between the sidewalk lines

so long as the light permits, so many people,
dozens right here in this city on their paths,
I, too, on my errands, so many of us

visible at the stroke of a single glance,
a phantasmagoria of humanity, more people
than I'd see in a year from the front porch

of a cabin on Deer Mountain in Ketchikan,
all of them perfectly shaved and heeled
appropriately, dressed in modern fashion,

and carrying their satchels of important things,
like me, each with a weight in his or her head
of the important thoughts, gold or lead,

such as when a boss said, "Maybe you are
better suited for a smaller company"
before she filed her own resignation

a few months later. Without ever realizing it,

some of us will change our own lives today
with a small act, it could be by calling an old friend,

or by walking down the other side of the street,
or by letting the mind wander to an impulse,
possibly tasting a dangerous one, that unsettles

the balance of ordinary and from that point on
you might find yourself seeing from the outside
your own body throwing off a lifelong capitulation

with a shrug as though undressing from an old cloak,
and wonder who you once were, and who you
have now, in this bright instant, just become.

Out to Sea

Maybe you, too, have felt it,
the tug of the bow line
hitched to your belly, pulling you forward,

away from the safety of the pier,
of the shore, away
from the curly-haired child

waving to you in first light.
Jacketed, bare-boned, hard-headed,
you went to sea

because life's an adventure,
because you were bent to discover
the one hard truth

every sailor learns in due time
by starlight, adrift among sea swells
in the middle of nowhere.

The solitude can toughen you
Or else make you mad.
You were not born to be alone.

Then, to return is divine,

is a salvation of fact, to know
you never had to leave, and yet,
of course, you had to, to know it.

Commitment

Scent of water,
taste of bread,
Yesterday, tomorrow,
What's said is said.

Feint of wind
And turn of phrase,
helping hands
To mend my ways.

Before it's settled
Dust to dust,
This dream I follow
Because I must.

Made in the USA
Columbia, SC
07 January 2022

53754664R00065